Pure freedom

Seven Secrets to Sexual Purity

An active, Bible-based
curriculum for young women

A ten-session retreat or Bible study

To be used with the book
And the Bride Wore White
by Dannah Gresh

DANNAH GRESH

Seven Secrets to Sexual Purity
Copyright © 2000
By Dannah Gresh

Pure Freedom
State College PA 16801
814-234-6072
www.purefreedom.org
dannah@purefreedom.org

All Scripture quotations are taken from the *Holy Bible, New International Version®*. NIV®. Copyright © 1973, 1978, 1984 by International Bible Society. Used by permission of Zondervan Publishing House. All rights reserved.

ISBN: 0-8024-8333-X

3 5 7 9 10 8 6 4 2

Printed in the United States of America

CONTENTS

a word from
DANNAH GRESH
(Dannah is pronounced like Hannah)

THE NEED

Why are you taking on this task? If you are like me, you have plenty to do with your precious time. So, why are you preparing to teach this Bible-based curriculum? I am betting that God has prodded your heart in a special way, and I would love to hear it, but let me give you a few good reasons for using your time in this way.

- *Eighty percent of teens say they are tired of the safer sex message and want more information on how to say no to sex.* I have seen young women come to Christ through this curriculum. They come because they are looking for some truth about sex. They come to know Christ because they see His great love for the very first time within the truth of sexuality. Wow!

- *A full 88 percent of girls say they have no problem dating someone of another religion. Sixty-nine percent actually have. Thirty-three percent of religiously active girls say they have no problem dating someone of another religion.* I don't have to tell you the long-term and sometimes lifetime heartache that can follow that kind of thinking.

- *Forty-three percent of conservative Christian teenagers say they have had sex by age 18.* Unfortunately, that does not demonstrate much of a difference between youth within the church and youth outside of the church. Shouldn't there be a difference? I think so! Obviously, you do too!*

The need is great for effective sex education to take place *within* the faith community. Despite positive steps toward more abstinence education within the public schools, adults still haven't begun to portray sex as an honored, beautiful gift and a portrait of love between a Savior and His bride, the church. That is something that can only take place within the church.

PURE FREEDOM PROVIDES PRACTICAL "HOW-TO" skills for aggressively developing and maintaining purity in a world stained with sexual pain. The retreat is presented in a fun two-day, one-night sleepover that the girls say is a blast! (Or you may opt to use it as a ten-week Bible study.) The seven secrets to sexual purity are presented in fifteen hours of an active curriculum using small group discussions, individual activities, group games, and fun object lessons. Every session carries a deep scriptural challenge to the attendees on an intimate level.

*Sources: *The Power of Abstinence* by Kristine Napier, Avon Books, 1996. *The Youth Ministry Resource Book* edited by Eugene C. Roehlkepartain, Group, 1988. *Right from Wrong* by Josh McDowell & Bob Hostettler, Word Publishing, 1994.

OUR OBJECTIVES

The retreat's primary *purpose* is to give young women practical tools to live a lifestyle of purity to the very day of their wedding. The retreat's primary *focus* is falling head over heels in love with JESUS! Our objectives are simple but powerful. The young women who attend will:

- Identify the difference between being innocent and being pure.
- Establish informal mentorships with select women who participate.
- Recognize the covenant purpose of sex as well as the earthly blessings that God rewards us with, if that covenant is protected.
- Write commitments to protect their love for God with undistracted devotion.
- Learn and practice refusal skills for questionable situations.
- Commit to keep God first and to save sex for marriage.
- Create a goal for a godly marriage by committing to date only Christians and by writing a dream list for their husbands-to-be.
- Write a letter to God, placing themselves and their struggles before Him.
- Worship the greatest love of their life—Jesus!
- Begin the process of healing from sexual sin if it exists in their lives.

OUR METHODS

Think back to important things you have learned in your life. Chances are, you learned by experience. My educational philosophy is that the most effective kind of learning is experiential. The least effective kind of learning comes about from verbal teaching. So, this curriculum uses three types of sessions, which emphasize experiential learning with limited verbal teaching. These three types include:

- **Alone Time**—The young women will work with their journals, their Bibles, and their personal copy of *And the Bride Wore White* during these times. The girls love it! I usually have to pull them away from their journals when time is up.
- **Small Group Workshops**—I like to tell them that this is really time for major girl talk! (Remember sitting around at sleep-overs and talking the night away?) While they use worksheets, their Bibles, and their copies of *And the Bride Wore White*, they will be talking about things like how they dress, what they dream of in a husband, and more. *The key is that this conversation is focused and guided by an older, godly woman.*
- **Large Group Challenges**—This is where *some* verbal teaching will be used, but even these sessions are often very interactive and require some careful planning to prepare. Take the time to read ahead and be ready. It will be worth it. These sessions will be powerful and God will bless your socks off!

Thank you for being a part of the effort to encourage young women to live a lifestyle of purity. I am praying Psalm 45:1 for you as I write this. It says, "My heart is stirred by a noble theme..." (Oh, that God would stir and stir your heart on the subject of purity!) "...My tongue is the pen of a skillful writer"! Let God do the "talking." You are just the pen! Isn't that relieving, but powerful? May God write on the hearts of the young women you lead to experience *Pure Freedom*.

Dannah

WHAT YOU NEED

This curriculum guide gives you the information you need to conduct the entire Pure Freedom retreat exactly as Dannah conducts it. You will have the option of using two videos with this curriculum. Purchasing these is strongly advised:

- Focus on the Family's "No Apologies" Video*
  Call 1-800-A-FAMILY
- The Medical Institute's "Just Thought Ya Oughta Know" Video*
  Call 1-800-892-9484

You will need to purchase:

- One copy of *And the Bride Wore White* for each attendee

GETTING READY

- **Plan your publicity** well in advance using the publicity materials and ideas beginning on page 7.
- **Gather a minimum of ten prayer warriors.** These women must commit to pray daily 30 days prior to and throughout your retreat. If you are conducting this as a ten-week Bible study, ask them to pray throughout the ten weeks, but especially on the days you meet. This is a vital part of your planning. Don't overlook it!
- **Gather one mentor—or burning flame, as we will call them—for every 5 to 10 attendees.** This is an older, godly woman who will attend and be involved with the young women. She will need to meet with you once to get an overview, but the small group guide sheet will carry her through each session quite easily. You will probably want to provide a copy of this guide to each mentor.

HOW TO USE THIS GUIDE

To get started, read over the brief **overview** at the beginning of each session. This overview will include *the objective* of the session, *the action* to be undertaken by each attendee, *the items needed*, and *the preparation activities* you must tackle. If you are planning this as a retreat, you will want to do this several weeks in advance so that you can enjoy the planning and take your time. If you are planning this as a ten-week Bible study, you should still read over the overviews collectively several weeks in advance so you can plan ahead for items that require some time to acquire.

Key Point:
Key points will show up in the margins like this.

Here's a good tip...modify the text as you feel God leading you. In most cases, I insert my story, but it would be really effective if you share yours when it seems appropriate.

As you plan more in-depth for each session, you will see that you can read through it and easily facilitate the session. For the speaking sessions, the session is written out as you would speak it. These are your speaking notes. Just highlight, write in the margin, have these with you, and you are ready to go. Here are some other helpful hints as you plan:

- Each session is designed to be approximately one hour in length. (If you are doing it as a ten-week Bible study, schedule an hour and a half so you have time to socialize.) You can modify that as you see fit for your group. Once you add in snack times, meals, and free time, the retreat is about 15 hours.
- Dive in and participate, and make sure that your mentors do too! Don't be spectators. This will make it more fun for you and more effective for the young women who attend.
- Don't tell the attendees in advance what you have planned. Keep everything as a surprise. At first, some may think the activities are a bit silly, but they will end up enjoying them and learning from them. Active learning isn't always comfortable, but it is memorable.

* Videos are used by permission of the producers. Use of these videos does not constitute endorsement by the producers. Use of the videos is at the discretion of the local facilitator.

How much publicizing you do will depend on what your plans are for your retreat. You may only send home an announcement to let parents know this is a part of your class for the next ten weeks. Or, if you conduct a community-wide retreat, you may publicize aggressively for a few months. Whatever you decide, we want your publicity efforts to go smoothly, so we provide several pieces to use in preparation. Your publicity pages include:

- Logo at the bottom of this page to cut out and copy as you advertise this event
- One church bulletin insert/handout
- One parent handout
- One prayer warrior letter

PLANNING PUBLICITY

All of the pieces can be photocopied in an effort to meet your publicity needs.

Some ideas for publicity from retreats in the past include:

- If you are doing a community-wide event, spend the majority of your time in one-on-one meetings with other youth leaders. If it is church-wide, spend the majority of your time in one-on-one conversations with potential attendees and their mothers.
- Send a woman to share in local churches/youth groups or Bible studies within your church.
- Request local radio stations to conduct a phone interview with you or Dannah Gresh during publicity.
- Have a breakfast for your prayer warriors and share more in-depth about the retreat. Word of mouth is always your best advertising.

PUBLICITY IDEAS

Don't forget to pray over the details of publicity.

LOGO

Pure freedom

Seven Secrets to Sexual Purity

Seven Secrets to Sexual Purity
Using *And the Bride Wore White* by Dannah Gresh

It's not just another sex talk.

"Thank you for teaching me about purity—something no one has ever set me straight on. I feel new, pure...like a princess. Now there is wisdom behind my actions instead of just following my parents' rules. That is so freeing."

-Carolyn, 16

"I have learned about sex in a different way, even after hearing typical 'no-sex' talks before. Thank you so much!"

-Maria, 15

Hey, girls! Did you know that most Christian women enter their teen years with a desire to remain sexually abstinent until their wedding day, but 42% of conservative Christian teens say they have had sex by age 18?* (Whoa! That's worth talking about, but *another* sex talk!?) **PURE FREEDOM: SEVEN SECRETS TO SEXUAL PURITY** is interactive and fun. It's not just another sex talk. It's about giving you usable tools to protect yourself. You will leave having answered these questions with fun interactive games, major girl talk, and videos:

- What is sex *really?*
- What are Satan's top sex lies?
- How can you stomp on them with God's glowing truth?
- Is it too late for me? How can I heal from mistakes I have made?
- What are the top **SEVEN SECRETS** among girls who make it to their wedding day? How can I use them in my life?

Pure Freedom is based on the book *And the Bride Wore White* by Dannah Gresh.

*Source: *Right from Wrong* by Josh McDowell & Bob Hostettler, Word Publishing, 1994.

This sheet is taken from Dannah Gresh, *Seven Secrets to Sexual Purity* (Chicago: Moody, 2000), and is used by permission.

Church Bulletin Insert/Handout

To Parents of Young Women
from the facilitator of Pure Freedom

DEAR PARENTS:

I hope you will aggressively encourage your daughter to attend *PURE FREEDOM*. Parents often see dramatic changes in their daughters after the daughters have participated in *PURE FREEDOM*. That is something only God can do, but I believe He is using this fun and unique approach. The girls who have attended *PURE FREEDOM* say it is a blast! Every interactive session carries a deep scriptural challenge to the attendees on an intimate level.

The young women who attend will:
- Begin informal mentorships with women who attend.
- Write commitments (for their eyes only) to keep sex out of their relationships until their wedding night.
- Gain a deep understanding of the covenant purpose of sex as well as the earthly blessings that God rewards us with, if that covenant is protected.
- Write commitments to protect their love for God with undistracted devotion.
- Develop a list of "Top Ten Comeback Lines" for questionable situations.
- Examine the way they dress, talk, and act to see if it is A-OK!
- Create a vision of a godly marriage by committing to date only Christians and by writing a "shopping list" of character qualities for their husbands-to-be.
- Write a letter to God, placing themselves and their struggles before Him.
- Worship the *greatest* love—Jesus!
- Begin the process of healing from sexual sin if it exists in their lives.

The retreat's primary *purpose* is to give young women practical tools to live a lifestyle of purity to the very day of their wedding. The retreat's primary *focus* is falling head over heals in love with JESUS!

As parents you are wondering how the retreat deals with sex. Honestly, we will deal far more with heart issues than specific issues of sexuality. One portion of the retreat discusses the truth of sexuality using two videos "No Apologies" by **Focus on the Family*** and "Just Thought Ya Oughta Know" by **The Medical Institute for Sexual Health***, a strong pro-abstinence organization. We also use chapters 13 & 14 of the book *And the Bride Wore White* by Dannah Gresh during this time. Feel free to contact me if you have any questions.

* Videos are used by permission of the producers. Use of these videos does not constitute endorsement by the producers. Use of the videos is at the discretion of the local facilitator.

This sheet is taken from Dannah Gresh, *Seven Secrets to Sexual Purity* (Chicago: Moody, 2000), and is used by permission.

seven secrets to sexual purity

To Small Group "Burning Flames"
Instructors for small group facilitation

Session #2 Purity Is a Process

Time: 15 minutes
Activity: T-Shirts
Purpose: to affirm each girl in your group
Materials: pen, colorful markers, paper

Ask each girl to draw a T-shirt for the girl on each side of her. The T-shirt should be representative of the girl's personality who will be "wearing it." For example, if the girl next to you is vibrant and the life of the party, but she is always kind and making people feel comfortable, you might draw a heart with confetti coming out of it and bright balloons in the background. Go around the circle and let each girl show her "T-shirts." Watch your time closely.

Session #4 The World's Sex

Time: 15 minutes
Activity: Discussion of "No Apologies" Video
Purpose: to clearly define the consequences of sexual sin

You will have just viewed "No Apologies," an excellent video by Focus on the Family. Let the girls discuss it. Some probing questions to get things going might be:
- What stuck out to you? Any faces? Comments?
- What were some of the consequences to not waiting until marriage to have sex?
- What was your opinion of the way some of the guys discussed sex?
- What are some of the benefits to waiting?

Session #5 Sexology 101

Time: 35 minutes
Activity: Researching Sex
Purpose: to clearly define sex according to the Bible
Materials: photocopied worksheets from session #5

Each group has its own different set of instructions for this session.

Session #6 Purity Is Governed by Its Value

Time: 30 minutes
Activity: Value Evaluations
Purpose: to discuss modesty and physical standards
Materials: photocopied Value Evaluations from session #6

Ask each girl to read page 76 beginning at "I've heard the saying..." and ending on page 78 at "escort them into the happily-ever-after." Pass out the Value Evaluations. Fill them out and discuss them. Finally, turn to pages 90–91 in the book. Using the chart on page 90, do steps 1, 2, and 3 on page 91 together.

Session #7 Purity Speaks Boldly

Time: 20 minutes
Activity: Top Ten Comeback Lines
Purpose: to practice refusal skills

Work as a group to complete the list of "Top Ten Comeback Lines" on page 101 of *And the Bride Wore White*. Let some be funny, but make sure some are God-focused. Bring your very best one back to share!

Session #8 Purity Dreams of Its Future

Time: 25 minutes
Activity: The Shopping List for Him!
Purpose: to build a vision of a godly husband
Materials: a special piece of paper for each girl

Give the girls time to write and think about their husbands—what he will be like, what he will look like, how he will act, what will be important to *him*. They may talk about it together. After about ten minutes, stop them and begin a brief discussion on "His Other Love." Read 2 Corinthians 6:14 together. Discuss that openly. It is important to push them, but they must do the deciding. Thirty-three percent of conservative Christian teens think it is OK to date non-Christians. Test this thinking!

Session #9 Purity Loves Its Creator

Time: 20 minutes
Activity: Pearl Necklaces
Purpose: to make pearl necklaces while measuring responses
Materials: monofilament, clasps, pearls

Provide materials to each girl to create her pearl necklace. Use this time to evaluate their need for counseling, as this session can be one that makes them tender.

Session #10 Purity Embraces Wise Guidance

Time: 35 minutes
Activity: What Momma Don't Know Won't Hurt Her
Purpose: to talk about communication with parents
Materials: poster board

Play the game "What Momma Don't Know Won't Hurt Her" in your small group. Your large group facilitator will explain the game before you break up. Give yourself 15 minutes for the game.
The main portion of this small group is to discuss just how hard it can be to talk about sex, or perhaps to communicate in general, with Mom. Your goal is to come up with three things that really make communication difficult, particularly in the area of sex. For example, "I wish my mom would bring it up more often." Then, come up with five usable ideas to fix those problems. For example, "As a teen, I need to take my mom out one evening and ask her to tell me about her dating years." At the end of this discussion you will have a poster board full of ideas to share with the other groups. Select one presenter from your group to share what you find in the large group.

If you are using this curriculum as a retreat, you may adopt this sample schedule or make one up on your own. The schedule can be kept fairly tight with little free time. They won't need it. They will feel like they are having free time throughout many of the sessions.

Most organizations need to schedule the retreat for a Friday evening and a Saturday, so this sample schedule was created with that in mind. This works well but requires that the majority of the information is provided to them on the second day...after they have just had a contest to see who can stay up the latest! If you can, start the retreat earlier on the first day and move a few more of the sessions to that day. Sessions 4 and 5 would be my recommendations to move to Day One.

Note that Session #3 works best if it is the closing session for Day One and Session #6 is a great mid-morning break for the girls on Day Two.

Day One

6:00	Registration, Welcome Time, Mentors greet and hug and talk to girls!!!!
6:45	Session One • And the Bride Wore White
7:45	Session Two • Secret #1: Purity Is a Process
8:45	Break, Snacks
9:15	Session Three • Secret #7: Purity Watches Burning Flames
	(This session should be planned as the closing session for the first day.)
10:15	Free time
	(This is a good time to counsel girls who demonstrated some need earlier.)

Day Two

8:30	Session Four • The World's Sex
9:30	Session Five • Sexology 101
10:30	Session Six • Secret #3: Purity Is Governed by Its Value
	(This session is a good one to have mid-morning, as it wakes them up.)
11:30	Session Seven • Secret #4: Purity Speaks Boldly
12:30	Lunch Break
1:30	Session Eight • Secret #2: Purity Dreams of Its Future
2:30	Break
2:45	Session Nine • Secret #5: Purity Loves Its Creator at Any Cost
3:45	Session Ten • Secret #6: Purity Embraces Wise Guidance
4:45	Closing Session
	(You might ask for testimonies at this time.)

Seven Secrets to Sexual Purity

Dear Prayer Warriors:

You have agreed to be the very backbone of the local *PURE FREEDOM* program. The program is based upon the book *And the Bride Wore White* by Dannah Gresh.

The program's primary *purpose* is to give young women practical tools to live a lifestyle of purity to the very day of their wedding. Its primary *focus* is falling head over heels in love with JESUS! Satan does not like this much, as you can imagine. But you have the authority to call for battle in the heavenly places on behalf of these young women. Will you do that with me?

Here are some specific prayer requests for the retreat.
- Pray for those who have registered by name, if possible, and as specifically as you can. Pray that the extra-busy lives of some of these students would not interfere with their attendance. Pray that each heart would be softened to hear from Jesus.
- Pray that the Lord would break through strongholds in their lives prior to the retreat so that their hearts are a fertile soil for the messages. (Pray specifically against existing impure relationships that serve as a barrier between the girls and Jesus.)
- Read Psalm 63. It can be considered "The Purity Chapter." Pray it in your own words: "Oh, God, You are MINE! I will search for Your presence every day with all my heart. My heart is only quenched by You and my body yearns to be with You..."
- Pray for me, your facilitator, as I prepare materials.
- Pray for the small group leaders who will attend for the weekend. They will have the chance to testify, and often their testimonies are powerful in the lives of the young women in attendance.

Thanks, again! The success of PURE FREEDOM really lies in the hands of our prayer warriors! I cannot wait to see what God will do through us.

This sheet is taken from Dannah Gresh, *Seven Secrets to Sexual Purity* (Chicago: Moody, 2000), and is used by permission.

Objective:

To exalt God as our Teacher, specifically in the area of learning to live a lifestyle of purity.

Action:

To write a letter to God, placing themselves and their struggles before Him.

Items Needed:

One used magazine for each girl (Make sure you have a few teen-oriented magazines that you
    might not normally have lying around. Ask around for them or purchase them.)

Pens and notebook paper for girls who forget them

Some soft background music for their alone time

Some fun contemporary Christian music

"Just Thought Ya Oughta Know" Video*

Preparation Activities:

    Read over the presentation text.

    Write your own letter to God the morning of this session.

    Pray! (Really pray. I usually do a prayer walk claiming the site and the girls for God just
prior to this session.)

AND THE BRIDE
WORE WHITE

*Who'll Teach Me to
Live a Lifestyle
of Purity*

SESSION 1
PreVIEW

SESSION 1 AT A GLANCE

ACTIVITY	MINUTES	WHAT ATTENDEES DO	SUPPLIES
Welcome	3	*Receive love from you*	
Ground Rules	2	*Hear the expectations for conduct*	
Game Time	15	*Play "The Magazine Game" to get to know each other and to begin to examine the world's view of sex*	*Magazines*
Video	15	*View and recall main themes in "Just Thought Ya Oughta Know," beginning to recognize some of the lies about sex that are prevalent today*	*Video*, Call 1-800-892-9484 to order*
Alone Time	25	*Read Chapter One in* And the Bride Wore White *and write a letter to God placing themselves and their struggles before him.*	

LESSON AT
A GLANCE

* This video should be previewed.
Some may choose to show it to
only senior high students. It
addresses some much needed subjects such as the ineffectiveness of
a condom and the fact that any
type of sexual contact is sex. Those
two truths are not taught in many
of the schools and in the media. It
is important to dispel the lies. If
you choose not to show it to some
or all of your students, use the
accompanying video booklet to
discuss these issues appropriately.

This is perhaps the most important session. Relax! It's also the easiest session. Just read over your text and be ready to have some fun with the girls.

WELCOME

▶ **Welcome Presentation • 3 Minutes**

Have fun contemporary music playing when they arrive. Greet each girl personally. Let the music play until you are ready to welcome them formally.

Tell the girls a little about why you felt led to be involved in this specific curriculum and what you feel God could do through it. Then say something like this:

> *I think you will find this to be a lot of fun. It was developed by Dannah Gresh, the author of* And the Bride Wore White.

> *During the course of our time, we will be either meeting in our large group like this, working together in small groups, or having alone time with your journals, your Bible, and your own copy of* And the Bride Wore White.

GROUND RULES

▶ **"Setting Some Ground Rules" Presentation • 2 Minutes**

> *If we are really going to get what God wants for us to get out of this experience together, we need to establish two important rules. I want to be able to tell you some of my most intimate thoughts and feelings, and I want you to feel absolutely free to do the same. So, our first ground rule is this…everything that is told stays within these walls. This rule is to protect the person sharing.*

> *The second ground rule is that there is to be no "mooning"! (Girls might giggle here! Let 'em!) You know what mooning is, right? You don't need me to show you, do you? Well, just like I don't really want to see your actual body parts…I don't want to see any mental images of your body either. So, when you talk with me or with the group or anyone individually, we don't need to see what happened with your body, but what happened inside of your heart. This rule is to protect those with whom you are sharing.*

Key Point:
Rule #1: Everything stays within these walls.
Rule #2: No mooning.

> *Pretty simple.*
> *Rule #1=Everything stays within these walls.*
> *Rule #2=No mooning.*

> *If everyone can agree to that, we can continue. This is very important. OK?*

GAME TIME

▶ **Magazine Game • 15 Minutes**

Give each girl one magazine and ask them to break into their small groups in corners of your main meeting room. (This may be the first time they are broken into small groups if you haven't taken care of this in earlier business opportunities. If it is the first time, move through it quickly.) Each group should be an equal distance away from a chair in the center of the room. For each round of the game, you will ask a specific girl a question about herself. (Try to ask each girl at least one question, but if you have a lot of girls, make sure to ask the less expressive girls questions.) Their answer is the item that everyone needs to try to find in the magazines in picture form or the exact word(s). When a girl finds an "answer," she rips it out and gives it to her mentor/burning flame. That woman runs it to the center chair. The first group to get their "answer" there wins a point for their team. (Sometimes you have to be a judge to determine either who was first and/or if the picture qualifies as a good answer.) At the end, the small group with the most points wins the game.

Sample Questions…

(Lauren), what is your favorite color?

_____, where did you last go on vacation with your family?

_____, what do you like to do in your free time?

_____, what is something that you like to wear every day?

_____, if you had a day alone in your bedroom, what would you do in there?

_____, what is your favorite dessert?

_____, what is your favorite subject to study?

_____, what is something you have done to make money?

_____, what is something that your friends do that you would never do?

_____, what flavor of ice cream do you like the most?

_____, what flavor of ice cream do you like the least?

After you've asked all or many of the girls questions, ask them to find these items:

Find a girl who looks ready to go on a date.

Find a guy who looks attractive.

Find an article that talks about sex.

Find an article that talks about abstinence.

After everyone has had a chance to answer a question and you've asked the few extras above, stop to count up the piles and determine a winner. You may reward the small group that wins with some chocolate Kisses or Hugs, if you like. Then, use the game to begin to open their minds to the fact that this world definitely distorts sex, and our mission is to discover God's undistorted truth. This will be a brief and probably inconclusive discussion time. Stay on schedule. You might start with the following discussion questions:

•How hard was it to find an article on sex? What about one on waiting…abstinence?

•What can you tell me about how the guys and girls look in these magazines? (Sexy? Alluring? Seductive? In many cases!)

•What about even some of the other subjects...innocent ones like vacations, desserts, studying, clothes...what messages do you see in those pages?

•What is the overall message these magazines and others like it give us about sex? Do you think these accurately portray God's message about sex?

Close the game time and bring them into a more worshipful attitude by praying and asking God to reveal His truth to the group about sex.

VIDEO

Video • 15 Minutes

Show "Just Thought Ya Oughta Know" if you have chosen to purchase it. (Call 1-800-892-9484.) This video aggressively addresses some vital issues, such as the ineffectiveness of condoms and the definition that any kind of sexual contact should be considered sex. With a growing trend among Christian kids to be involved in oral sex, this is an issue that needs to be addressed in an appropriate and intelligent manner. *If your group is young or well-sheltered from public school sex education, you may find this video too intense to use. It uses terms such as "mutual masturbation," "oral sex," and "anal sex."* If you do not use it and discuss it briefly, you might invite a medical professional to share some truthful information about risks associated with sexual sin.

ALONE TIME

Alone Time • 25 Minutes

I'd like to now present each of you with your own copy of And the Bride Wore White. *We are going to read through some of the book throughout this retreat, but you'll have lots of chapters left to explore on your own when we are done.*

Hand out *And the Bride Wore White*

During all of our alone times, I will be playing worship music for you. When the music changes from a quiet, worshipful music to something louder and more fun...that is your signal to move back into the large group. Close up your time with God and move quietly back into the large group area. For this alone session, I would like you to read all of Chapter One. At the end of the chapter, the author will ask you to write a letter of your own.

RETREAT If you are doing a weekend, intensive retreat...you will go immediately into Session #2 now.

WEEKLY STUDY If you are doing a ten-week session...please take the remaining time to close in prayer within your small groups. Let this session end quietly and pensively. End with a large group announcement..."This week, continue to write that letter to God every day. Start over every day if you need to, but really take your struggles to Him. Next week, I will have some very freeing thoughts for you as we discover Secret Number One in the seven secrets to sexual purity!"

Objective:

To define purity and to differentiate it from innocence.

Action:

To draw a picture of the thing that most keeps them from pursuing purity in their life and to place that at the cross of Jesus.

Items Needed:

A large bundle of pens or pick-up sticks

Chris Rice CD "Deep Enough to Dream" to play the song "Clumsy" (Optional)

A piece of glycerin soap with a spiral symbol in it for each girl (Optional)

A large poster board

One large roll of postal paper for each 15 girls and colored markers

Photocopies of "Crosses" reading at the end of this lesson

Preparation Activities:

Read over the presentation text. You will teach a lesson in this session.

Read chapter 6, page 43 in *And the Bride Wore White.*

Prepare poster board with spiral for a visual aid during your presentation.

Photocopy the "Crosses" reading.

SESSION 2 AT A GLANCE

ACTIVITY	MINUTES	WHAT ATTENDEES DO	SUPPLIES
Game Time	10	Play "Chinese Numbers" to learn to look past the obvious.	A bundle of pens or pick-up sticks
Large Group Challenge	25	Learn a three-step definition of purity, accentuating the difference between innocence and purity.	"Deep Enough to Dream" CD by Chris Rice (optional), poster board, spiral glycerine soap for each girl (optional)
Alone Time	10	Draw graffiti representing their struggle with lust vs. purity. Prayerfully place that before Christ.	Postal paper, colored markers, "Crosses"
Small Group Workshop	15	Hear words of encouragement from fellow small group members.	Paper and colorful markers

GAME TIME

Chinese Numbers Game • 10 Minutes

Chinese Numbers is a game that teaches us to look beyond the obvious…to think outside of the box. Tell the girls that you will make a "Chinese" number on the floor, being careful not to say that you will be using your bundle of pens or pick-up sticks. They are to guess what the number is as they discover how the numbers are made. They should not tell the others how it is done. Give them time to discover it. Look efficient, and carefully lay four to ten of the pens in a chinese-number-looking pattern. Then, subtly lay your hands to your sides or to the sides of your pattern on the floor so that all of the girls can see them. You will be making the actual number with the number of fingers you have extended. If you want to make a three, lay three fingers casually on the floor with the rest curled under your hand. Let them guess what your Chinese number is. After a few numbers, give them the clue that "all of the numbers have been one through ten because that is all you can make with what you have here." As girls begin to get it, invite them to make the numbers for the group, taking turns so several of them get it. Toward the end of your time limit, take over again. This time, be clumsy and drop the pens onto the floor and obviously place your fingers next to the numbers. Make sure that each of them sees how it has been done, explaining it if needed. End by saying, "Sometimes you have to look beyond the obvious for the truth of a situation. Let's see if we can do that right now with the subject of purity."

LARGE GROUP CHALLENGE

Large Group Time • 25 Minutes

If we are going to study PURE sex, we've got to start with a thorough understanding of what purity is. Turn to Philippians 2:15. God desires "…that you … BECOME blameless and pure."
Read Philippians 2:15 again, emphasizing YOU! Make it personal to them from Jesus!

Play "Clumsy" by Chris Rice (Optional)

Can I ask you something? Do you ever really feel like that—like you've totally missed the mark? Like you've just messed up the perfection that God started with when you were born? Like you have contaminated the goodness He created in you? Maybe it is something small and silly that makes you feel inferior. Maybe it's a huge secret, sexual sin that keeps you cowering in your walk with God. Memories can be more convicting than any judge or jury.

I went through a real period of struggling with my own purity when…(Insert a mini testimony here.) I felt like I'd really messed up. Let's test those feelings against Scripture for just a second…

In And the Bride Wore White, *Dannah uses Kaye Briscoe King's Spiral (Show the spiral you've drawn on poster board) upon which she says we "travel" our life's journey, hopefully ending in the dead center of the spiral where we have become truly Christlike. Stick with me on this. It gets a little deep, but this knowledge is really freeing.*

•Point Number One—I was not born pure. "Surely I have been a sinner from birth, sinful from the time my mother conceived me" (Psalm 51:5). "There is not a righteous man on earth who does what is right and never sins" (Ecclesiastes 7:20). OK, you weren't born yesterday, so you can handle this…YOU WEREN'T BORN PURE. You were innocent when you were born, but those Scriptures say you were born sinful. So, any notion that you have "lost" your purity is nonsense. You may never have had it. I know women who've got some yucky stuff in their past, but whose lifestyles exude purity. And, I know young women who think they are pure in a very technical sense, but whose lifestyles are anything but pure. Innocence is where you begin and it is possible that you have lost some of your innocence, but purity…that's where you end up! (Point to the center of the spiral!)

Key Point:
I was not born pure.
Psalm 51:5

•Point Number Two—In Luke 17:1a Jesus says that things that cause people to sin are bound to come! So, it is a given. I will face the monster of lust in my life. (Draw a scary lust monster across the first line of your spiral.) *It might come in the form of being tempted to use language that robs you of your testimony, it might come in the form of being tempted with an eating disorder, or it might come in the form of being tempted to give your heart or your body away in a relationship. Temptation is inevitable. It is not a sin in itself…this is the exciting part…facing that is a chance to pursue purity. Each of us was born with Lust hanging around. The dude is just sitting there waiting for us to get to him. As we choose to journey toward a close relationship with God, he rears his ugly head.*

Key Point:
I will face the monster of lust
in my life.
Luke 17:1a

One of three things will happen when you meet Lust. You'll breeze past him with God's help. Or he'll taunt and tease you pretty effectively…maybe causing you to sin…but you eventually struggle past him. Or you just get stuck there with him for a long, long, long time.

Hopefully, you're one who makes it past him and says, "Whew! Made it." And you journey on. But suddenly one day, you notice (because you are walking in a spiral) that there he is again. He doesn't look quite as scary because you have seen him before, but you think, "No way! I fought with you before. You're a part of the past." But there he is and you have to go on.

(You may insert your own mini-testimony here or use mine.) This happened to Dannah Gresh once. She talks about being home all alone at 11:00 at night. She let herself get fooled into thinking that she needed to watch "90210," thinking that it was "research" for her book. That show got her

feeling desires, thinking thoughts, dreaming dreams…none of which were A-OK! Since her husband was on a trip, she crawled into bed alone and thought, "I am either going to fantasize myself to sleep or I am going to tell Lust no!" She prayed, "God, I'm too sleepy to fight this off. Help me, please! I have seen this monster before and he doesn't look so big and scary anymore, but I could easily play his game tonight."

Let's read something together. Turn to page 40 in And the Bride Wore White. *Let's read that first paragraph to the bottom of the little lizard graphic.* (Read or have a good reader read the C. S. Lewis "red lizard" story out loud.)

Key Point:
I can become pure.
Philippians 2:15

•*Point Number 3—Anyway, back to the spiral. The good news is that each and every evil dude we face on our journey can, like C. S. Lewis's little red lizard, be completely transformed. And as you make right choices, that wimpy little beast turns into something wonderful for God. Kaye Briscoe King says that purity is the opposite of the sin of lust.* (Extend the line of that first little monster. At the opposite end of the ugly face, draw an angelic face with a halo to represent purity.) *So, as you confront lust and make right choices with the help of God and friends and lots of fast, strategic exits, that little monster, Lust, slowly becomes a contented, uncompromised companion—Purity.*

In And the Bride Wore White, *Dannah writes, "I felt so relieved when I first had the Spiral explained to me. You see, I felt so guilty for always running into Lust. He was smaller and his roar less threatening each time, but he kept showing up. The fact that he showed up to taunt me, I learned, was not my sin—it was a given and a chance to walk deeper into the Spiral and closer to my dear God if I said 'no' to lust. Purity is a process. What a freeing secret…*

  •*I was not born pure.*
  •*I will face the beast of Lust, perhaps over and over again, but that in itself is not a sin. Rather it is a chance to develop my purity by talking to God, talking to a friend, and making a fast, strategic exit.*
  •*I can become pure."*

I think it is really important that you grasp this. Understand that you are probably going to run into this guy, Lust, most of your life. Be ready for him and know that saying no to him is what pushes you in that direction toward purity.

Understanding that purity is a process is the first secret toward living a lifestyle of purity and to experiencing a fantastic sexual union with your husband.

Let's just challenge one another to pursue purity. Look inside yourself right now. If there were a little red lizard on your shoulder, what would he be called...

>*•An unfaithful mind...one that fantasizes?*

>*•Too many movies that get your mind wandering from a pure lifestyle?*

>*•Maybe God is tugging at your heart to give up a relationship that is not holy?*

>*•Maybe you've still not received healing and forgiveness for sins in your past?*

Understand that you can BECOME pure. God desires that YOU become pure!

Alone Time—Graffiti Wall • 10 Minutes

(Prior to the session, have someone spread out the postal paper and scatter markers, crayons, and colored pencils across it. Also spread out copies of the "Crosses" reading.)
Play a CD of worship music while you talk and while the girls do this activity. The object is to do this as alone time even though they will be all together. There should be no talking.

I want you to close your eyes and visualize that little red lizard in your life. Everyone has something. All of us...the mentors included...are going to do this. What is that red lizard in your life? It could be just a lack of enough alone time with God to make you pure, or it could be outright sex that rips at your heart. Think of that right now.

Now let's all quietly walk over to the brown paper on the floor. I want us to each quietly draw some graffiti there that represents that red lizard and how it makes you feel.

(Give the girls 8 to 10 minutes to draw and color.)

Now, I would like you to grab that picture you've just drawn and rip it out in the shape of a cross and come stand in a circle here with the little poems I have placed in a circle.

(Give everyone a chance to get in the circle with their crosses as well as a "crosses" reading.) Take this time to read the prayer committing these struggles to God. Tell Him that you are symbolically tearing the struggle into the shape of a cross to recognize that the power of the cross can overcome the struggle. Invite the girls to say their own one-sentence prayers. You may close in a personal prayer.

Small Group Workshop • 15 Minutes

It is important to really affirm these girls again and again...to make them feel their real value in Christ rather than the value that PMS, bad-hair days, and peer pressure can place upon them. In your first small group workshop, we are going to invite the group members to affirm one another in a fun way. This is a good close to the definition of purity because some girls may have just been thinking about mistakes they have made. They need to know they are valuable in God's eyes regardless of what sins they have committed.

ALONE TIME

SMALL GROUP WORKSHOP

Sit in a circle. Ask each girl to draw a T-shirt for the girl on each side of her. The T-shirt should be representative of the girl who will be "wearing it." For example, if the girl next to you is vibrant and the life of the party, but she is always kind and making people feel comfortable, you might draw a heart with confetti coming out of it and bright balloons in the background.

After everyone has had a chance to draw T-shirts for the girls on each side of them, take turns going around the circle and let them present them as they explain to the group what they mean. This is a great way to encourage each other and get your small group started off in a positive manner.

Presentation of Gifts—Spiral Glycerine Soap • 3 Minutes
(Optional, but very effective! Spoil 'em and show 'em God's tender love for them! This soap is easy to find. The spiral soap is a popular soap. If you cannot find it, don't worry. It is a nice touch, but not necessary.)

> *I want each of you to have a gift from me and the other mentors here. We have a small visual symbol to remind you that you can BECOME pure. What is inside that gift? Yes, spiral soap! Remember that God desires to cleanse you and make you pure!*

CROSSES READING:

COPY AND CUT OUT ONE FOR EACH GIRL. YOU WILL PRAY THIS TOGETHER AND SHE CAN TAKE IT HOME AS A MEMENTO.

CROSSES

Leader: Lord, when we look at these tattered crosses,

Group: We are reminded that You endured the pain of our punishment so that we do not have to hold on to our pain.

Leader: Lord, when we look at the shape of these,

Group: We can be sure that You know what our pain feels like since You bore it on the cross.

Leader: Lord, help us to bring our pain and sin to You. Help us to learn to forgive ourselves as You have forgiven us. Help us to replace our shame and fear with certainty and peace.

Group: Change our hurting to healing. Show us once again that when You say You forgive us You truly mean that You were given for us.

Leader: Amen.

RETREAT   If you are doing a weekend, intensive retreat…you will take a break to change into pj's and have a snack. Depending on your start time, you may determine to have free time here.

WEEKLY STUDY   If you are doing a ten-week session…have each mentor give her girls big hugs to end the evening. Following the hugs, make a large group announcement: "Next week, you will have the chance to hear the honest and candid testimonies of the mentors here. You don't want to miss their stories as they will give you courage!"

Objective:

To begin to strengthen the relationship between the attendees and the mentors and to convince them that a mentor is important in their lives.

Action:

To worship the One who must be the greatest love of their life—Jesus—and to hear the testimonies of women who exemplify that love today and who are currently pursuing purity.

Items Needed:

One inexpensive votive candle for each girl

Matches

Lyrics to favorite worship songs (Choose some related to loving God and purity)

Worship CD(s) if you do not have a worship leader

Preparation Activities:

Read chapter 16, pages 149–53 in *And the Bride Wore White.*

SESSION 3
PreVIEW

SESSION 3 AT A GLANCE			
ACTIVITY	**MINUTES**	**WHAT ATTENDEES DO**	**SUPPLIES**
Large Group Worship Time	15	*Worship the greatest love of their lives—Jesus!*	*Worship leader or CDs, candles*
Alone Time	10	*Read chapter 16 of* And the Bride Wore White.	
Large Group Worship Time	5	*Worship the greatest love of their lives—Jesus!*	*Worship leader or CDs*
Large Group Challenge	25	*Listen to the testimonies—including those of virginity/innocence and those marked by sin—of mentors who are currently pursuing purity.*	
Large Group Worship Time	5	*Worship the greatest love of their lives—Jesus!*	*Worship leader or CDs*

LESSON AT
A GLANCE

LARGE GROUP WORSHIP

Worship Time • 15 Minutes

You may select one of the mentors with musical talent or bring in a woman with special musical talent for just this session. Guitar music or something informal would be nice. If you don't have a guitar, consider some great worship CDs, as the instrumentals add a lot to the worship experience. Worship time should focus on loving God and pursuing purity. Choose songs the girls can relate to and enjoy singing. Open with having each mentor hand each girl in her group a candle and lighting it. Each mentor should say, "This represents your burning flame!" You might set a few larger candles throughout the room for brighter candlelight, as they will be reading lyrics. (Note: You may want to save the "burning flame" candles to use again for session 10.)

ALONE TIME

Alone Time—M.O.R.E. • 10 Minutes

I would like you to take your candles and spread out in this room for just a few moments of alone time. Turn to page 147 in And the Bride Wore White *and read Dannah's story about how she became a burning flame…and how very much she needs burning flames in her life.*

LARGE GROUP WORSHIP AND CHALLENGE

Worship Time • 5 Minutes

Continue the attitude of worship with one or two more songs by candlelight.

Testimonies of "Burning Flames" • 25 minutes

Each burning flame should have about 3 to 5 minutes to tell her quest for purity and how she pursued it in her life. It might be that she did not always pursue it, but she is aggressively pursuing it today. IT IS VITAL THAT YOU HAVE SCREENED YOUR BURNING FLAMES BEFOREHAND TO BE SURE THAT YOU HAVE AT LEAST ONE WOMAN WHO IS A VIRGIN OR WHO WAS A VIRGIN ON HER WEDDING DAY. This woman's role is to share a vibrant, exciting testimony of how the wait has been worth it. She must demonstrate that it can be done! Don't hide the testimony of others who have sexual pain in their past. Often it is these women whom the girls feel most comfortable confiding in.

Worship Time • 5 Minutes

Continue the attitude of worship with one more song by candlelight. Invite the girls to stand in a circle and thank God for the testimonies they have just heard. Ask them to be sure to hug each mentor and to enCOURAGE her, because what she has just done may have been difficult.

RETREAT   I encourage this to be the last session of the evening, even if you have to reorient the order of the sessions. Send the girls off to bed with this worshipful attitude. Many of them may continue sharing deeply.

WEEKLY STUDY   If you are doing a ten-week session, end with this announcement: "Next week, we are going to hit the subject of sex hard. Don't miss it as we begin to give you some concrete reasons WHY you should wait until you are married to enjoy the blessings of sex."

THE WORLD'S SEX

Gathering the Truth
About Sexuality

Objective:

To identify the lies Satan tells us about sex and to develop the ability to intelligently combat them with medical, emotional, and spiritual truth.

Items Needed:

Small Nerf basketball hoop (Or a toddler's floor hoop)

A marble for each girl

A large ball that will sit on the rim of the hoop, but will not go into it

Some chocolate candy kisses

Preparation Activities:

Review the "No Apologies" video.

Read chapter 2, pages 21–25, in *And the Bride Wore White* and prepare a summary.

SESSION 4
PreVIEW

SESSION 4 AT A GLANCE

LESSON AT A GLANCE

ACTIVITY	MINUTES	WHAT ATTENDEES DO	SUPPLIES
Large Group Challenge	5	*Hear a brief summary of chapter 2 from* And the Bride Wore White	
Game Time	5	*Play a game that demonstrates the risk associated with sexual activity*	
Video	30	*Watch "No Apologies," which showcases the testimonies of three girls who experienced the consequences of sexual misuse.*	*The "No Apologies" Video, Call 1-800-A-Family*
Small Group Workshop	20	*Discuss what they learned in regard to the opinions of teens about sexual activity, the risks of early sexual activity, and the benefits of abstinence.*	

LARGE GROUP CHALLENGE

Introduction • 5 Minutes

BRIEFLY summarize chapter 2 from *And the Bride Wore White*, leaving out any information about the human papilloma virus.

GAME TIME

Game Time—How Safe Is That? • 5 Minutes

(Hand out the marbles. Set up the basketball hoop to be about five feet away from a foul line.) *Let's start this session out with a little contest for some candy kisses! I have given each of you a marble. I want each of you to approach this foul line and "dunk" your marble and then take this large ball and try to also dunk it.* (They may giggle because they can already see visually that the ball will not fit. As each girl takes her turn, count how many marbles go in and how many times the larger ball sits on the rim.) *Congratulations, you all just had sex with a condom.* (Number of big balls that went in) *of you got pregnant.* (Number of marbles that went in) *of you got an STD. And all for a kiss!* (Hand out kisses to all of the girls.) *OK, this was just a game, but let's see what we can learn from it. Condoms were created to do what?* (Some might say to prevent STDs. This is incorrect. They were created to prevent pregnancy. Make sure you let them answer until they get the correct answer.) *So, we have something that was created to prevent pregnancy. It does this RELATIVELY effectively since this was its intended use. The microscopic holes in a condom are smaller than sperm and if it is used correctly, it usually does not break. But condoms were not created to prevent STDs. Have you heard of HPV? Human papilloma virus? It is the fastest spreading STD today. It is gross and uncomfortable because it causes genital warts. But more frightening, it causes 90 per cent of all cervical cancer, so it is also deadly. Do you know how much protection a condom offers you against HPV?* (Let them offer an answer.) *NONE! A condom will not protect you against this common **AND DEADLY** STD. How safe is that?*

Key Point:
The human papilloma virus causes 90% of all cervical cancer. A condom provides no protection against HPV.

VIDEO

"No Apologies" Video • 30 Minutes

Play the video. It is strongly recommended that you purchase and use this video. It is appropriate for middle school through young adult age groups.

SMALL GROUP WORKSHOP

Small Group Discussions • 20 Minutes

You will have briefed the small group mentors to discuss the video. They should ask questions such as "What stuck out to you this evening? What were some of the consequences to premarital sexual activity?" Let them list all of them, but make sure they include the emotional issues...pain, regret, embarrassment, shame, a broken heart.

RETREAT Move quickly into the next session!

WEEKLY STUDY If you are doing a ten-week session, end with this announcement: "This week we looked at consequences, but I'd like to know...isn't there a benefit to waiting? There are, in fact, at least three of them that are very worth waiting for. Come back next week to discover what they are!"

Objective:

To recognize the covenant purpose of sex as well as the earthly blessings that God rewards us with, if that covenant is protected.

Action:

To research and learn about sex according to God's Word.

Items Needed:

Four large, colorful poster boards or foam core boards

Colored markers, crayons, colored pencils

Old magazines

Lots of three-dimensional scraps such as yarn, old keys, coins, pasta, beads, etc.

Preparation Activities:

Read chapters 13 (pages 127–32) and 14 (pages 135–40) in *And the Bride Wore White.*

Divide the small groups into four groups even if you have more or fewer than four

small groups. Determine which group will do each small group activity. The options are:

- It's a blood covenant! (Choose a mature group to do this one.)
- It's a blast!
- It enhances intimacy!
- It's for baby-makin'! (A good one for the younger attendees.)

SESSION 5 AT A GLANCE

ACTIVITY	MINUTES	WHAT ATTENDEES DO	SUPPLIES
Large Group Challenge	5	Read aloud from pages 127 & 128 in And the Bride Wore White *and receive research assignments*	
Small Group Workshop	35	Dig deeply into chapters 13 and 14 of And the Bride Wore White *and discuss one of four specific parts of the biblical definition of sex. Prepare to present findings to the large group.*	Poster boards, pens, etc.
Large Group Challenge	20	Collectively define sex as a covenant which portrays the greatest spiritual truth we know and which is an "if/then" agreement offering blessings in three specific forms.	

LARGE GROUP CHALLENGE

Introduction • 5 Minutes

Read aloud or have good readers take turns reading aloud *And the Bride Wore White* page 127, beginning with *"How can I even start to rearrange the meaning of sex in your mind?"* Read through page 128 to *"Please stop to pray earnestly for God to speak to you."*

Take a few quiet minutes to commit this teaching time to God. Invite Him to be our Teacher. Give the attendees some open prayer time to utter one-sentence prayers to God. Close the prayer time.

You are now going to move into your small group (or explain how they will be divided so that there are four groups). *You are going to do your own research there and come back to report to the large group what you have learned about the definition of sex according to God.*

SMALL GROUP WORKSHOP

Small Group Workshop • 35 Minutes

Each group has its own different set of instructions. They will basically be digging into and discussing Chapters 13 and 14 in *And the Bride Wore White*. Each will be assigned to one portion of the "If…then" agreement. They will then be preparing a presentation on their poster board to teach their truth to the rest of the large group.

LARGE GROUP CHALLENGE

Large Group Time • 20 Minutes

Beginning with "It's a blood covenant," let each group discuss what it has learned. Be sure to have thoroughly read the chapters and fill in any key thoughts or verses they have left out so that the entire group understands the whole concept. Give the first group a full five to seven minutes as they have the most information to share. Break the time up between the other three groups. During this time, be sure to read aloud pages 130 through 131 where *And the Bride Wore White* explains the Jewish wedding ceremony and compares it to the love of Christ for His bride, the church.

Take a few quiet minutes to thank God for teaching you during this time. Again, offer attendees time to utter one-sentence prayers of thanks for specific things they learned. Close the prayer time.

RETREAT   Take a fifteen-minute break to prepare for the next session. Ask the attendees to come back in a calm state of mind. Tell them to bring pillows and blankets to get comfortable.

WEEKLY STUDY   If you are doing a ten-week session, end with this announcement: "You don't want to miss next week's session. Dannah says it is everyone's favorite. Be sure to bring a pillow and a blanket with you."

Sexology 101

Group #1

"Sex Is a Blood Covenant!"
Yours is the most important of the four purposes of sex. Dig deeply and be prepared to "teach" this wonderful spiritual truth to the rest of the group just thirty-five minutes from now!

Assign each of the verses to one or two members of your group to read.

Proverbs 2:17 • Romans 12:1–2 • Matthew 25 • Ephesians 5:31–32

- •1 What does Proverbs 2:17 call marriage?
- •2 What does Romans 12:1–2 beg us to consider our bodies to be?
- •3 As Jesus talks about the ten virgins, what is He really explaining?
- •4 What great spiritual "mystery" does Ephesians 5:31–32 say the sexual union represents?

Read the rest of Chapter Thirteen in *And the Bride Wore White*.

Be prepared to summarize it to your small group and the large group. You may choose to read any parts that are significant to you.

- •1 Specifically what kind of covenant is the sexual union? (p. 129)
- •2 What evidence was expected of a bride to prove she was a virgin? (p. 129)
- •3 What is the hymen? (p. 130)
- •4 What is portrayed through marriage according to Jewish wedding customs? (pp.130–131)
- •5 What kind of agreement is a covenant? (p. 132)

When you rejoin the large group, you will be given the opportunity to share this great truth in 5 minutes or less.

Sexology 101

"Sex Is Great Fun!"
Yes, that is part of what God intended. If we experience sex as God intended, it is blessed in three ways. This is the first of them!

Assign the key verse to a group member to read.

Proverbs 5:18–19

"Captivated!" Don't you just love that word? Don't you love the idea of being the object of one man's desire to the point of CAPTIVATING him? God can do that. It comes from part of the blessing. What does that mean to you?

Read the section marked "Sex is Great Fun" (pp. 136–137) in Chapter Fourteen of *And the Bride Wore White*.

Be prepared to summarize it to your small group and the large group. You may choose to read any parts that are significant to you.

•1 What does *Redbook*'s survey prove about God and sex?
•2 What did Greg Johnson say in "What Hollywood Won't Tell You?"

When you rejoin the large group, you will be given the opportunity to share this great truth in 3 minutes or less.

Sexology 101

"Sex Is for Baby-Makin'!"
OK, that's pretty much as basic as it gets, huh? If we experience sex as God intended, it is blessed in three ways. This is the second of them!

Assign the key verse to a group member to read.

Genesis 1:28a

•1 What does God command us to do in this verse?
•2 So, what purpose does the act of marriage fulfill?

Read the section marked "Sex Is for Making Babies!" in Chapter Fourteen (pp. 137–138) of *And the Bride Wore White.*

Be prepared to summarize it to your small group and the large group. You may choose to read any parts that are significant to you.

•1 How does it affect you to think that God creates a life from two microscopic cells?
•2 How does it make you feel to think that you will probably one day experience this great miracle within your body?
•3 How do you think the experience of having a baby before you were married would compare with having one after you were married?

When you rejoin the large group, you will be given the opportunity to share this great truth in 3 minutes or less.

Sexology 101

"Sex Enhances Intimacy!"
If we experience sex as God intended, it is blessed in three ways. This one is too amazing!

Assign the key verses to group members to read.

Genesis 2:24, Ephesians 5:31–32

•1 What does Genesis say we become when we are married?
•2 What word does Ephesians use to describe the level of intimacy a
marriage should have?

**Read the section marked "Sex Enhances Intimacy" in Chapter
Fourteen of *And the Bride Wore White* (pp. 138–140) and read
pages 131–132.**

*Be prepared to summarize it to your small group and the large group. You may choose to
read any parts that are significant to you.*

•1 What is sex meant to be a portrait of?
•2 What responsibility does that place upon us to protect it?
•3 How could we harm the intimacy with our future spouse if we are
sexual with others now?

When you rejoin the large group,
you will be given the opportunity
to share this great truth in 3 minutes
or less.

PURITY IS
GOVERNED BY
ITS VALUE

*Discovering and
Demonstrating
Your Value
in God's Eyes*

Objective:

To discover their value in God's eyes and to determine to present themselves based upon it.

Action:

To be treasured and loved by you and the other mentors so that they sense God's love and to evaluate their own habits in the areas of communication, dress, behavior on dates, and exposure to impure things.

Items Needed:

One fine china tea cup per girl (This MUST be a delicate, precious cup, not church-pantry quality ceramic. You might consider buying them and giving them as gifts to the girls. I do. They love them!)

A flavored tea and sugar (I use Raspberry Royal by Bigelow)

Gourmet cookies (I use Pepperidge Farms Milano and Raspberry Chantilly)

Fine chocolates such as Godiva (if you can swing it) or Ferrero Rocher (more affordable)

Hand lotions in popular scents

Preparation Activities:

Read Psalm 45 along with chapters 8 and 9 in *And the Bride Wore White*.
Read over presentation text. You will present a challenge in this session.
Photocopy the "Value Evaluation."

Large Group Tea Party • 20 Minutes

SESSION 6 AT A GLANCE

ACTIVITY	MINUTES	WHAT ATTENDEES DO	SUPPLIES
Large Group Tea Party	20	Be treated to a delightful tea party and a relaxing hand massage	A CD, tea party supplies, hand lotions
Large Group Challenge	10	Discover God's value as verbalized through Psalm 45 and be challenged to use that as their compass, not bad hair days and hormones	Pillows, blankets to rest quietly
Small Group Workshop	30	Discuss how they can demonstrate God's value through the way they talk, dress, the places they go on dates, and what they expose themselves to on a daily basis	A photocopy of "Value Evaluation" for each attendee

LARGE GROUP TEA PARTY

The purpose of this tea party is not just to have fun, but to lavish these girls with God's love. It is important that it is well-planned and that things go smoothly so that the girls can just relax. Your mentors or adult volunteers should have the tea and cookies ready in ANOTHER room. (This should come as somewhat of a surprise for the girls! For one reason, they might think they are too old...for another, the surprise makes it all the more special for them.) It is generally best to prepare the tea in one large pot and ladle it into cups just before serving so that it stays hot. Cookies and chocolates should be presented on lovely platters with doilies. Add your own ideas to make it absolutely top-quality pampering.

Start a CD of calm, "tea-party" instrumental music playing in the background. Invite the girls to spread out and relax. They may cuddle into their pillows or lie down. Ask them to just listen to the calming music and to prepare to be pampered.

The mentors who are serving tea should begin to ladle it into the cups now. The remaining mentors should begin giving each girl a wonderful hand and arm rub using the scented hand lotions. As each girl is rubbed, just talk to her about herself. Tell her the ring she is wearing is lovely or that her hair looks nice today. Compliment her as you comfort her. Also, pray silently for her that God would cause her to feel His love.

LARGE GROUP CHALLENGE

Large Group Challenge • 10 Minutes

When all of the girls have been served tea and have received a hand massage, just listen to them for a while. You are ready to begin your challenge presentation when you see most of them have finished their tea and you hear one or two saying something like, "I feel so relaxed," "That was fun," or "Wow!"

Key Point:
God is enthralled by your beauty.
Psalm 45:11

How do you feel? (Let the girls respond.) *I hope that you feel treasured and precious and priceless because YOU ARE! Now, I know that a bad-hair day or an extremely emotional day or even your friends can make you FEEL quite the opposite, but our FEELINGS are not a good indicator of our value. Let's look at what God says. Just relax into your pillow while I read to you some of Psalm 45. First, let me tell you, Psalm 45 was written as a wedding psalm. It is a romantic story of a princess marrying her king. But it was also meant to be a portrait of Christ's adoration and love for you and me...the bride of Christ. Listen to what God says about YOU.* (Read verse 11.) *"The king is enthralled by your beauty; honor him, for he is your lord." Do you hear that? God looks at you and He is enthralllllllled by your beauty. What else does He say about you?* (Read verses 13–14a.) *"All glorious is the princess within her chamber; her gown is interwoven with gold. In embroidered garments she is led to the king." All glorious are YOU, the princess. God looks at you and sees a precious princess. God knows you. He formed you. He knows you better than you know yourself. Do you trust your Creator to be a better judge of your value than hormones and peer pressure? Just relax and listen to the music and think about how precious you are in God's eyes.* (Give the girls about two minutes to just enjoy the quiet solitude as the music plays.) *OK, now. Let me ask you something. What was really so great about what we gave you just now...the little tea party?* (Let them comment!) *Oh, come on, now. All we really gave you was some dead tea leaves in hot water. What is so special about that?* (Let them comment.) *Ah, it was the WAY I presented it to you that made it have value, wasn't it? There are three ways I could have presented these dead leaves to you.* (Hold up a styrofoam cup.) *I could have given you a styrofoam cup that was trashable when we were done. Would that have been as special? No, you'd throw that cup away when we were done, right?* (Hold up a simple, ceramic mug.) *OR, I could have just grabbed some every day ceramic mugs. We could have had a chatty time with those warm mugs, but I doubt we would've cared much to talk about them when we got home. BUT* (hold up one of the china cups) *if I give you the tea in these precious china cups with doilies, fancy cookies, and a hand massage...well, now you have a memory that you want to treasure and keep around, right? Ladies, it is all in the presentation. That is what made it valuable.*

I wonder. How do you present yourself? We know you are more valuable than those tea leaves and that you are a priceless princess in God's eyes, but how do you present yourself to the world around you, and especially to guys? Are you trashable styrofoam? (Show the styrofoam.) *Are you an every day old mug...OK if you are here OR if you are not?* (Show ceramic mug.) *Or, do you present yourself in such a treasured way that you are like a valuable piece of precious china? I would like you to go to your small group and talk about that.*

Small Group Workshop • 30 Minutes
In small groups, ask each girl to quietly read page 76 beginning at "I've heard the saying 'Every great love story ends in tragedy...'" and ending on page 78 at "... into the happily-ever-after." Pass out the Value Evaluation forms that were copied from this guide book. Give each girl a few minutes to fill hers out and then discuss them. In what areas are they trashable styrofoam, common ceramic, priceless china? Based on their own evaluation, are they headed for the "crash and burn" or the "pure, slow burn"?

Finally, turn to pages 90 and 91 in *And the Bride Wore White*. Using the "chart" on page 90, do steps 1, 2, and 3 on page 91 and discuss them aloud.

Move quickly into the next session!

If you are doing a ten-week session, end with this announcement: "Next week, we'll play the role of being a guy and getting crazed about Y-O-U! OK, what would you tell that Y-O-U-crazed guy when things are getting out of control? Find out next week!"

Key Point:
God looks at you and sees a princess.
Psalm 45:13–14a

Key Point:
How do you present yourself? As trashable styrofoam, an ordinary ceramic mug, or priceless china?

SMALL GROUP WORKSHOP

RETREAT

WEEKLY STUDY

Pure Freedom ❧

VALUE EVALUATION

So, are you presenting yourself as a styrofoam cup, a ceramic mug, or valuable china? It can be hard to decide without pulling apart your behavior moment by moment. In each instance below, check how you evaluate yourself.

	STYROFOAM CUP	CERAMIC MUG	VALUABLE CHINA
THE WAY I DRESS			
THE WAY I TALK ABOUT GUYS WITH FRIENDS			
THE WAY I TALK TO AND WITH GUYS			
THE PLACES I AM WILLING TO GO ON DATES			
THE THINGS I AM WILLING TO DO ON DATES			
THE THINGS I TALK ABOUT ON DATES			
HOW EAGER I APPEAR TO GUYS			
THE TIME I SPEND WITH GOD TO LET HIM DIRECT DECISIONS ABOUT MY DATING			

Take the time to look at your answers above and decide whether you are headed for the "Crash and Burn" or the "Pure, Slow Burn." Circle the one you are headed toward. Then finish the sentence in the space provided below.

▶ Based on my own evaluation, I think I am probably headed for the "Crash and Burn." Here is what I need to change...

▶ Based on my own evaluation, I think I am probably headed for the wonders of the "Pure, Slow Burn." Here is why...

PURITY SPEAKS
BOLDLY

*Preparing Your
Tongue for Dates*

Objective:

To learn and practice refusal skills.

Action:

To think of their own refusal phrases and to use them in a fun game.

Items Needed:

One large poster board or chalkboard

Two folding chairs

Preparation Activities:

     Read chapter 10 (pages 95–101) in *And the Bride Wore White.*

SESSION 7
PreVIEW

SESSION 7 AT A GLANCE			
ACTIVITY	**MINUTES**	**WHAT ATTENDEES DO**	**SUPPLIES**
Alone Time	10	*Read chapter 10 of* And the Bride Wore White.	
Small Group Workshop	20	*Come up with a small group list of "Top Ten Comeback Lines" for when things get out of control physically. Select one or two to share so that the large group has a top ten list.*	*Pens and books*
Large Group Challenge	10	*Have fun sharing the top ten comeback lines for your group!*	*Poster board or chalkboard*
Game Time	20	*Practice using refusal skills as written in the top ten comeback lines.*	*Two folding chairs*

LESSON AT
A GLANCE

ALONE TIME

Alone Time • 10 Minutes

Play some fun instrumental music softly as you allow girls to spread out in a common area to read chapter 10 in *And the Bride Wore White*. Now is a good opportunity for you and the small group leaders to pray for the girls by name. (Take as many opportunities as you can to do that! After all, it is all about what God can do *through* you.)

SMALL GROUP WORKSHOP

Small Group Workshop • 20 Minutes

Working as a group, complete the list of "Top Ten Comeback Lines" on page 101 of *And the Bride Wore White*. Let some of the answers be hilarious and fun, but make sure a few are God-focused and serious.

LARGE GROUP CHALLENGE

Large Group Challenge • 10 Minutes

Have fun with this session. Invite everyone to offer a "drumroll" as you count down the "Top Ten Comeback Lines for (name of church or group) women!"

GAME TIME

Game Time • 20 Minutes

This game is called "Freeze!" because the object of it is to do just that when passion gets out of control. This is really a fun way to build confidence and help girls to remember that they CAN refuse advances and HOW to do just that!

I want to see just how (name of church or group) women put those top ten comeback lines to use! So, let's play a fun game of "Freeze!" I am going to invite two of you at a time to sit in these chairs. I'll start with (name of a fun, extroverted mentor or attendee). Since I am on the left, I am the girl. The girl sitting on the right will always be the "guy." Those of you watching get to make up situations that I truly hope you never find yourselves in. The "guy" and girl on this date have found themselves in a position where the guy's passion has been ignited, and it's up to the girl in this case to cool things off. The "guy" gets to come on to the girl until she verbally refuses him in a way that convinces the rest of you. When she uses one of our comeback lines or another great one she has made up, everyone scream "Freeze!" We'll give the girl the chance to be the guy and move another one of you into the girl seat! Are ya ready to play "Freeze!"? (Encourage cheering and hollering. This game depends on it!) Let me hear you!

(Some sample scenarios include in a car at lookout point, at a movie theater in the back row, watching a video alone in your house, etc. The "guy" might come on verbally or by touching her suggestively on the legs or making an attempt to reach over her shoulders, etc.)

RETREAT   Invite the girls back into the large group for the beginning of session eight.

WEEKLY STUDY   If you are doing a ten-week session, bring the girls back into the large group for a closing prayer time. Invite them back to dream about their husbands-to-be next week. Next week they will also learn about a three-step plan to getting impurity out of their lives.

PURITY DREAMS
OF ITS FUTURE

*Envisioning a Godly
Husband*

Objective:
To develop a vision for the future that includes a godly Christian husband and that will encourage attendees to live a lifestyle of purity.

Action:
To write a "shopping list" of qualities for their husband-to-be.

Items Needed:
A few dozen tennis balls
A special sheet of colored paper for each girl to write her list
Two cups of white glue
3 tsp. Borax detergent
Warm water

Preparation Activities:
Read over presentation text. You will present a challenge in this session.
Read over the directions to make "gluep."

**SESSION 8
PreVIEW**

SESSION 8 AT A GLANCE

ACTIVITY	MINUTES	WHAT ATTENDEES DO	SUPPLIES
Game Time	15	Play a game where they don't want to get "caught with the odd ball."	A few dozen tennis balls
Small Group Workshop	25	Write a "shopping list" for their husband-to-be. Close in a time of prayer for their husband-to-be.	A sheet of special paper for each girl
Large Group Challenge	20	Learn a three-step plan for breaking off sinful relationships in an effort to protect the dream and to watch a visual demonstration of how God desires to be a part of that plan.	Materials to create "Gluep"

**LESSON AT
A GLANCE**

GAME TIME

Game Time • 15 Minutes

Ahead of time, you will have marked one of the tennis balls with a dot using a permanent marker. The girl who has this one at the end of each round is out of the game.

We are going to play "Don't get stuck with the odd ball." I am going to give several of you three balls each.

(Give every second or third girl three balls.)

When the music begins to play, begin tossing them one at a time to someone who does not have any balls. When the music stops, freeze. Anyone with balls needs to check to see if she has this "odd ball."

(Show them the ball with the tiny mark on it.)

If you have this "odd ball" you are out of the game.

(Play the game until only one person is left the winner.)

You got stuck with the odd ball because in this game, you could not be choosy about which balls you got. You got what was thrown your way and you accepted it as a part of the game. That's not how you should date. You could get stuck with an odd ball. If you aren't carefully analyzing each guy that comes your way, you won't really know what you are getting. I want to read you a letter from one of Dannah's friends. This letter is from a real woman who wrote this just for you.

To a dear sister:

I want to tell you a little story. When I was a senior in college, I met a guy who "talked the walk," but did not "walk" it. He knew all the right Christian lingo and how to push all my buttons. We became very close way too fast. I fell head over heels for this good-looking guy. Things went too far, and we had sex. I was so ashamed. I always wanted to wait for the man I would marry, so when he asked me to marry him (after only three months) I said yes. In my heart, I knew things weren't like they were supposed to be.

No one thought the relationship was right, but I kept convincing myself that everything was OK. This man was older and irresponsible. He also had a very bad temper. He hit me before we got married, and it only got worse and worse afterwards. Because of my lust for a handsome man and a sexual relationship, I made the worst mistake of my life.

After about a year of marriage, God provided a way of escape for me by exposing what this man was doing to me to other people. I had some support to help me through and it was obvious that he did not think anything was his fault and would not change. With Scripture and counsel, I felt that it was necessary to get out of the relationship for the sake of my life. I did get out, but the scars of that relationship linger with me today. I even made more mistakes after my divorce because I did not realize how deep God's forgiveness goes. I have found out that it is common for a girl who has made sexual mistakes to make more and more and more because she loses her self worth.

I think since we don't know each other, it's not even necessary for me to try to make myself look any better by sharing where things went after that tragic divorce. God has taken care of me, but I would not go through that again for anything in the whole world. Eventually God helped me see how deeply He loves me no matter what I do. When I finally realized God's love, I did not care if I ever got married again and I was able to begin to live a lifestyle of purity!!! It was so overwhelming and satisfying to know that His love was so deep. Please don't take the chance of ruining your life, or a big part of it, by giving up your purity. And please, please, please don't think that some guy who talks the Christian talk is truly living for God. Look at his life. . . . Was he living for God before he knew you? . . . Is he living for God when you are not around? . . . Do his friends want to live for God, too? Don't settle for anything less than someone who is totally sold out for God. If you want a more fulfilling, awesome marriage, wait until you find the person God has already appointed for you. And then, wait until you get married to share the incredible union of sex. You both will be fulfilled and walking in God's blessing!

Love in Christ,

A.

This young woman went through a period of just grabbing any guy who came by, and it cost her dearly. Perhaps if you know what you are looking for, you can save yourself a lot of hurt and heartache and it may give you the confidence to wait patiently.

(Summarize some of the key points you see in chapter 7 at this time. Especially spend time on information that falls under the "Personality Plus" and "His Other Love" categories.)

Let's dream! Move into your small groups to write a "shopping list" for him.

Small Group Workshop • 25 Minutes

In small group time, you will just give the girls time to write and think about this in a casual, fun atmosphere. They may discuss parts of their dreams as they work. After ten minutes, stop them and begin a brief discussion on "His Other Love." Read 2 Corinthians 6:14 together even if it was read in the large group setting. Discuss that openly. It is important to push them, but they must do the deciding. Thirty-three percent of conservative Christian teens think it is OK to date non-Christians. Test this thinking by asking them things like, "What happened to the woman in the letter? Did she think her boyfriend was a Christian? Perhaps he was. Is being a Christian enough, or should you be looking for something more?" End the small group time in quiet prayer for the girls' husbands-to-be.

SMALL GROUP WORKSHOP

LARGE GROUP CHALLENGE

Large Group Challenge • 20 Minutes

As the girls arrive in the large group, play quiet music and invite them to read chapter 5 of *And the Bride Wore White*. Invite them to write in their journals as they complete the reading. (The book instructs them to do this on page 49.) With five minutes left, you will stop them and make the gluep. The recipe for gluep is as follows:

In a large clear bowl combine:
1 ½ cups warm water
2 cups of white glue

In a second, smaller container combine:
1 ⅓ cups warm water
3 tsp. Borax laundry detergent

Mix ingredients in each container thoroughly. Pour contents of smaller container into larger container. Gently lift and turn the mixture until only a tablespoon of liquid is left. Gluep will be sticky for a moment or two. Let excess liquid drip off then gluep will be ready!

You will make the recipe *as you talk,* making an analogy between the glue and the sin in our life and the Borax and God's Spirit working in the midst of the sticky stuff! You should start with the two bowls of warm water.

> *Everyone here can probably name some little bit of impurity that they need to take through that three-step process of asking God for an undivided heart, telling a friend, and making a fast, strategic exit. I don't know about you, but asking God for an undivided heart can be really hard for me. I sometimes feel like I need to get my life all neat and cleaned up before I deserve to go before Him. Ever feel like that? (Oh, there are those feelings again!) Well, let's just test that against Scripture once again. This glue represents the sin in our lives. Tell me...what are some of the sins or sticky things that are in our lives on a daily basis?* (Let them name things like boyfriends, R-rated movies, pornography on the Internet, gossip, peer pressure, etc. Each time they name one let some of the glue ooze into the larger bowl of warm water. Once all of it is in there, stir it around good.) *That sticky stuff gets all mixed into our lives and it looks impossible to get it out, don't you think? What did we learn about asking God for an undivided heart? Does He expect us to come before Him after we have everything all neat and clean?* (They should answer no. He asks us to come to Him first.) *That's right. He wants to be invited right into the middle of that stuff. This is the Holy Spirit in powder form.* (Hold up the Borax in a clear cup and

smile! Pour it into the smaller bowl and mix thoroughly.) *God wants us to invite the Holy Spirit right into all of our life, not just the clean part.* (Pour the Borax mixture into the larger bowl.) *When we do, suddenly even the sticky things in our lives become pliable, usable, moldable. God can use even the sticky stuff if we invite Him into the middle of it.* (Lift the mixture out and let the water drip from it as you knead it with your hands. When all of the excess water is drained, hand it to the girls around you to pass around.) *Let's really commit to inviting God into the sticky stuff so He can work through it to make all of us moldable and usable in His hands!*

Play some fun, upbeat music as the girls play with the gluep. Let them have about five minutes to chat and play right where they are before you begin session nine.

RETREAT

Close in prayer and play some fun, upbeat music as they talk and leave. Invite them to return for the interactive session on loving God that they will never forget!

WEEKLY STUDY

**PURITY LOVES
ITS CREATOR AT
ANY COST**

*Pursuing a love rela-
tionship with Jesus*

Objective:

To let go of sinful relationships or any impurity in their lives and to commit to love the Lord Jesus Christ with all of their hearts and souls.

Action:

To write a love letter to God and to symbolically exchange a cheap price tag for a real pearl.

Items Needed:

One photocopy per girl of the price tag at the end of this lesson

One photocopy per girl of the love letter sheet at the end of this lesson

One real pearl for each girl (These can be purchased by the strand at most jewelers for nominal fees. They do not need to be high quality, but it really is important that they be real.)

Two feet of monofilament and one set of necklace clasps for each girl (These are purchased at any craft store and are very inexpensive.)

Preparation Activities:

> Read over presentation text. You will present a challenge in this session.
> Photocopy the price tags and prepare them as directed.
> Photocopy the love letter sheets.

**SESSION 9
PreVIEW**

SESSION 9 AT A GLANCE			
ACTIVITY	**MINUTES**	**WHAT ATTENDEES DO**	**SUPPLIES**
Large Group Challenge	10	*Learn the truth of the Pearl of Great Price.*	*A copy of one price tag for each girl*
Alone Time	20	*Write a "love letter" to God committing to Him the "fake pearls" they cling to and seeking to love Him.*	
Large Group Challenge	10	*Write the name of their fake pearls on their price tags and symbolically exchange it for a real pearl.*	*One pearl for each girl*
Small Group Workshop	20	*Make pearl necklaces and discuss their commitments with their small group.*	*Monofilament and necklace clasps*

**LESSON AT
A GLANCE**

LARGE GROUP CHALLENGE

Large Group Challenge • 10 Minutes

I only know one thing that is free, and that is God's loving forgiveness. But there is a very short parable in the Bible that Jesus told about a pearl of great price. I am sure you have heard it before. The entire little story goes like this...

(Read Matthew 13:45–46 from your Bible.)

That story says that to really pursue God, know God, and love God may require selling all that you have. It may cost you everything. I have a price tag for you.

(Pass the price tags out.)

Read that price tag with me. It says, "Everything costs something. One Thing costs everything." Everything does cost something. I want to tell you a few true stories.

Sara was an average Christian teenager just a few years ago. Unfortunately, she was tempted by lust and found herself in a relationship where she did not say "no." Today, Sara is not with us anymore. She contracted the human papilloma virus, which eventually turned into cervical cancer, and she died just a few years ago. Her sister approached Dannah once after she spoke and specifically asked that her sister's story be told. Sara's romantic desires cost her life.

Kathie is a middle-aged woman who once was a mentor at a Pure Freedom retreat. She is a vibrant Christian and the mother of three boys. Kathie came to be a mentor at the retreat because had she not had an abortion when she was a teenager, she would have been able to bring her daughter to that very retreat. Protecting her prideful and selfish name has cost Kathie a lot of tears for a lot of years and the loss of a dream...the dream to have a little girl.

Melinda is a college student preparing to go overseas to be a missionary. She has not dated seriously much, and all through high school she kept her mind and heart and body pure. She was very proud of that. She took a job at an Internet cafe where she was in charge of monitoring computers. Once she found some pornography on one of them and was lured into exploring the site. She soon found herself frequently looking for pornographic sites in the privacy of her dorm room. She cannot stop. Her grades have failed, she has lost several friendships, and she spends much of her time and money exploring pornography. She did not mean for it to happen, but she is addicted and now needs professional help to stop. A few moments of leaving her guard down and a lack of discipline for brief moments of pleasure have cost Melinda greatly. The cost of getting out by telling someone and getting help seems too much. The cost of staying in is also more than she is willing to pay.

Oh, you might not have stories like these where you have pursued the fake pearl of physical impurity, but what about your heart? You know you can be physically and sexually pure but still have a very impure heart. Look at Abraham and Isaac. The love between a father and a son would, it seems, be a pure and wholesome love. But God called Abraham to sacrifice it. Why? Because that love reigned in the place where God was supposed to reign unchallenged.

Key Point:
Everything costs something.
One Thing costs everything.
Matthew 13:45–46

Key Point:
God wanted to see whether
Abraham's love for Isaac reigned
where God should have, so Abraham
was called to sacrifice it.

If you read Dannah's book, you see that she faced that same kind of struggle. Her relationship with Bob Gresh was completely physically pure, but she found herself giving the reign of her heart to Bob rather than to God. You see, even "good" things can be fake pearls if they haven't had time to be cultured into the real thing. How did Dannah know that Bob was reigning in her heart? She started to make easy, heart-driven choices like holding his hand instead of reaching for her Bible in church or standing up friends when Bob called at the last minute. What did she do? Let's look. Turn to page 105 in your book.

(Read the beginning narrative of chapter 11.)

Have any of you ever broken up with someone? You know how much it hurts. At this point, Dannah had really thought she would marry Bob, but she did not know if she would get him back. She says she felt deep depression and hopelessness at first. So did Bob. Let's look at page 108.

(Read Bob's journal entry marked by the cherub.)

You can see that Bob was noticing also that he found himself at a place where there were no "deep roots of God" in his life. He had become dependent upon Dannah. They both began returning to God and inviting Him to once again reign in their hearts. Was it easy? Let's look at some of Dannah's journal entries from that time.

(Read the dated journal entries on pages 108 and 109.)

During this time, Dannah attended a Sunday school class taught by Bob. They were still not together, but their hearts were healing and they were becoming stronger in the Lord. In the class, Bob read Matthew 13:45–46, which says, "The kingdom of heaven is like a merchant looking for fine pearls. When he found one of great value, he went away and sold everything he had and bought it." His journal from the night before outlined his message that day. It read, "The Lord has taught me much in reading His Word tonight. They can be summed up in five statements:

> *1. There is a pearl of great price.*
>
> *2. We are to seek it.*
>
> *3. We are commanded to purchase it.*
>
> *4. It costs us everything.*
>
> *5. It is worth the price.*

"I must come to the point where I stop the payments on the fake pearls in my life and start making the payment on the real pearl. God costs everything. He is worth the price."

Bob had come to realize that if he wasn't willing to relinquish all the fake pearls in his life, he would never fully understand the blessing of God's goodness.

What are the fake pearls in your life? Please believe me that the sacrifice of them is worth the cost. What God can give you is so much more valuable. There is a story about a little girl who wanted

Key Point:
You must stop making payments on the fake pearls and start making payments on the Pearl.

pearls for her birthday. One year, she begged and begged until she got a simple strand of fake pearls. She loved those pearls. She wore them every day and talked often of them. One year, on another birthday, her daddy looked at her and asked her to relinquish the pearls. She hesitated. Her daddy asked her to trust him. She still hesitated. "When you are ready," said the daddy lovingly and turned to go. But the little girl ran to him and with tears in her eyes placed that simple strand of fake pearls into his hands. The daddy smiled and pulled out of his pocket a shiny, lustrous strand of real pearls and placed them on her neck. "I just needed to see that you would trust me," said the daddy.

God is like that. He never asks us to give something up that He does not return something better to us. It may not be the same form or even the same thing, but eventually we come to find the treasure in being willing to give up anything for the Creator who loves us so very much.
What are your fake pearls? I am going to play some music now and ask you to be in an attitude of prayer as you write a love letter to God, giving Him the fake pearls in your life.

ALONE TIME

Alone Time • 20 Minutes

Pass out the love letter handout if you have not already done so. Play some soft background music to create a buffer between the girls and to create an attitude of worship. Spend this time praying for the girls and ask that your mentors do the same.

LARGE GROUP CHALLENGE

Large Group Challenge • 10 Minutes

When you have finished your letter, I want to invite you to give at least one of those fake pearls you wrote about a name. Write that name on the price line of your price tag. Then, if you are truly ready to relinquish that fake pearl in your life to God, I want you to bring me that useless, cheap price tag and exchange it for a real pearl.

At this point open a nice jewelry box or a lovely box of some type and hold it in your hand. Stand there quietly as you wait for the girls to finish and to come to you. Once all or most of the girls have come to you to exchange price tags for pearls, close the session in a prayer committing the price tags to God. Ask the girls to continue in this attitude of worship as they move into their small groups. This can be a tender time for some, and it is important to maintain the quiet.

SMALL GROUP WORKSHOP

Small Group Workshop • 20 Minutes

Provide each small group with enough monofilament and clasps for each girl to create a necklace. They usually do not need any instructions to do this. They will each create a very in-style pearl necklace on monofilament. During this time, the small group leader can be sensitive to what is happening in her group. If one girl needs attention, the leader can move off to be alone with her. If not, she should invite them to discuss what they have just learned and been through with God.

RETREAT   Plan a break at this point in the retreat so that girls who need counseling can receive it.

WEEKLY STUDY   Close in prayer and be available for girls who would like counseling. You need to have read ahead to next week's lesson and be prepared at this time to invite mothers if you plan to do so.

FOR SALE

everything
    costs something

one Thing
    costs everything

$ _____

Pure freedom

purity loves its Creator at any cost

FOR SALE

everything
    costs something

one Thing
    costs everything

$ _____

Pure freedom

purity loves its Creator at any cost

Price Tags

Photocopy onto bright paper. Cut out and use a hole puncher to create a hole over the white circle in the black box. Place raffia, yarn, or string through the hole and tie to finish.

This sheet is taken from Dannah Gresh, *Seven Secrets to Sexual Purity* (Chicago: Moody, 2000), and is used by permission.

 **LOVE LETTER TO GOD**

purity loves its Creator at any cost

If you have a hard time obeying God in the area of your physical love life, it may be because you do not love Him.

John 14:21 says, "Whoever has my commands and *obeys* them, he is the one who loves me. He who loves me will be loved by my Father, and I too will love him and show myself to him."

In *Experiencing God*, Henry Blackaby says that *if you have an obedience problem, you have a love problem.* If you are struggling to obey God in the area of your physical love life, it may be because you do not love God.
If you really come to know God as He reveals Himself to you, you will love Him. If you love Him, you will believe and trust Him. If you believe and trust Him, you will obey Him.

Do you love Him? Take time right now to write Him a love letter. Explain to Him where you are in your struggle to stand pure before Him. Tell Him you are sorry if you have failed. Praise Him if He has kept you shielded from worldly passions. And specifically request Him to be your Teacher.

Only He can teach you to live a lifestyle of purity.

Much of this page has been adapted from:
Henry Blackaby & Claude V. King, *Experiencing God*

This sheet is taken from Dannah Gresh, *Seven Secrets to Sexual Purity* (Chicago: Moody, 2000), and is used by permission.

**PURITY
EMBRACES WISE
GUIDANCE**

*Inviting your
parents into your
dating relationship*

Objective:

To convince the girls that they can and must invite their parents into their dating lives (and
to give them an opportunity to do that if you opt to invite mothers to this session) and to
help them develop creative ways to communicate more effectively about dating and sex.

Action:

To develop ideas to improve communication between them and their parents, especially in the
area of sexuality.

Items Needed:

Paper and pens for small group workshop

One poster board and markers for each small group

One potato and one straw for each girl

Preparation Activities:

Read over presentation text. You will present a small challenge in this session.
Decide to invite mothers or not and prepare reminders or invitations.

**SESSION 10
PreVIEW**

SESSION 10 AT A GLANCE

	MINUTES	WHAT ATTENDEES DO	SUPPLIES
Large Group Challenge	5	Be welcomed lovingly. (If opting for mothers to attend, welcome moms!)	
Small Group Workshop	35	Play a game to break the ice if mothers attend or to just have fun even if mothers have not attended.	Pens and paper for each girl (and mother)
		Develop a list of three difficulties in communicating with Mom and Dad about sexuality. Develop a list of five ideas to make it easier.	A poster board and markers for each group
Large Group Challenge	20	Share their best ideas for better communication with Mom and Dad. Learn why that is so important.	Candles from session #3, potatoes, straws

**LESSON AT
A GLANCE**

In this session, you will be seeking to convince the girls that they really must invite their parents into their dating lives if they are going to be successful in living a lifestyle of purity. If you are using this as a ten-week Bible study, I encourage you to invite the mothers to be a part of this session. Invite them several weeks in advance, but send reminders or new invitations the week of this session. If you invite the mothers, you need to collect the candles from session #3 or purchase new ones for the mothers.

If you are conducting this as a retreat, I do not recommend that you invite mothers simply because the girls are really winding down and are low in energy by this last session. It seems to be more effective in the retreat setting to issue the challenge directly to the girls and to have the mentors follow up in the weeks to come by asking the girls if they have talked to their moms.

LARGE GROUP CHALLENGE

Large Group Challenge • 5 Minutes

Welcome to the last session of Pure Freedom! Everyone give someone next to you a big hug! You have learned sooooo much and made so many great decisions. Congratulations.

There's just one really important question to answer. "What's Mom got to do with MY sexual purity?" Even stranger to some, "What's my dad got to do with it!?"

Let's start with Dad. Let's get right to the point. Girls who lack a positive father/daughter relationship are very much at risk to be sexually active. David Blakenhorn in a book entitled Fatherless America *wrote, "Many studies confirm that girls who grow up without fathers are at much greater risk for early sexual activity, adolescent childbearing, divorce and a lack of sexual confidence." I don't want to go over a lot of statistics, but it seems that hugs from Dad keep us girls from overly craving hugs from guys. Your dads need to fill that guy-shaped hole in your heart. Hmmm? That can be tough. It really is true that "men are from Mars and women are from Venus." I see it every day in the father/daughter relationship. Don't you? How do we fix that? We will talk about that today.*

What about your mom? (Refer to her at this point and tell her you are glad she is here if she, in fact, is!) Well, she is really important in a way you might not even imagine. You see, we tend to relate to other people the way our mother does. Maybe it is because we see it reflected in her marriage or her personality today and it rubs off on us. Maybe it has to do with the Bible's reference to generational tendencies. But the point is this: you can learn from your mom's experience so that you can make strong and wise decisions in your own dating life. But how do you do that comfortably? Well, today is all about that. Let's break into our small groups and do some talking!

Small Group Workshop • 35 Minutes

For small group time, you will move all of the girls into their regular small groups. (If you have mothers attending, you will work with them as a group during this time. They will play the same games and discuss the same topics, but not WITH the girls. It will be more effective if they can talk freely about the "other" group and their struggles to communicate.)

Give yourself 15 minutes for this game. *The large group facilitator will describe how this game works before you break off into groups.* You must move quickly to get it completed. (You will start out with an ice-breaker to relax the mothers if you have invited them.) This is also a nice relaxer if you are doing a retreat format and do not have mothers around. The game is called "What Momma Don't Know Won't Hurt Her!" Each girl will write down four things about herself. Three of them will be true but very unusual. For example, here are some strange BUT TRUE things girls have said at retreats. "I was a published writer in second grade! I have a blue spot on my butt! I once colored my hair green! I have never been out of this state." One of the four things they write will be false, but the object of the game is to get other people to think it is true. Some false statements have been things like this: "I flunked my first driver's test! I don't use deodorant! My dad was born in the Bahamas!" Once everyone has had time to write four statements about themselves, each person reads their four and everyone writes down the one they think is false. That girl gets points for everyone she tricks. The girl at the end who has tricked the most people wins!

The main portion of this small group workshop is to discuss just how hard it can be to talk about sex, or perhaps to communicate in general, with a mom (or with a daughter). Your goal is to come up with three things that really make communication difficult, particularly in the area of sexuality. Then, come up with five usable ideas to fix those problems. It is great to have one or two ideas that would be for the other group. For example, "I wish my mother would bring the subject of sex up more often" (or "I wish my daughter would take a deep breath and just act like she is listening when I try to talk to her about sex"). BUT make sure that the majority of ideas are for self-improvement. "As a teen, I need to take my mom out one evening and ask her to tell me some of her dating adventures. I think that would help me trust her more" (or "As a mother, I think I need to write my daughter a long letter outlining my hopes and dreams for her in the dating and purity arena"). At the end of this twenty-minute discussion, you will have a poster board full of ideas to share with the other group. Here are some probing questions to make this session go smoothly.
- How often do you and your mom (daughter) discuss sex or dating? Is that enough?
- What happens when you and your mom (daughter) discuss sex or dating?
- Do you enjoy discussing this topic with your mom (daughter)?
- What do you wish your mom (daughter) would do differently?

SMALL GROUP WORKSHOP

• What about your dad? What do you wish he would do differently to be involved?

• What really frustrates you about how you and your mom (daughter) communicate?

• What are some things you have done in the past that have really helped? (Letter writing, dates with dad, confiding in mom, etc.)

• What do you think your mom (daughter) wishes you would do differently?

• What is one goal you can set right now to do in the next week that will improve communication with your mom (daughter), specifically in this area?

When you have only five minutes left, be sure to warn everyone and tell them so you can finish up their poster. Select one presenter to give a brief, two-minute review of your poster board when you return to the large group.

(If you have been working with the mothers, hand each her daughter's candle or a new one. Explain what the burning flame is and tell them that you will be talking about that in the large group session. When you signal them, each will simply go to her daughter and give her the candle and sit beside her.)

LARGE GROUP CHALLENGE

Large Group Challenge • 20 Minutes

Invite each small group to share their poster board in two minutes or less.

Tell a brief testimony here of how your mother played a vital role in your sexual purity or how you wish she had or you wish she had let you. You may ask another mentor to do this. The point is to convince the girls that they need to invite their mothers into their dating lives. At the end of this testimony, explain the role of a burning flame (chapter 16, page 147 for review). (Invite the mothers to bring their candles to their daughters, if mothers are attending.) Issue a challenge to the girls to sit down with their mothers within the next week and to light that candle and talk about sex and dating very candidly.

In closing, give each girl a potato and one straw. Ask her to push the straw the whole way through the potato. (It CAN be done, if you follow through with the movement and don't stop. A swift continuous motion will do it. Practice in advance so that you can demonstrate.) Though this is a short object lesson, it drives home a vital point! They must follow through with what they have learned. Encourage them to finish reading the book or to start journaling consistently or to invite a woman to be a burning flame for them or to do whatever God puts on their hearts. Give them a few minutes to reflect on what they need to do to follow through with this retreat. Finish the retreat or ten-week study with an open testimony time. Ask girls to share the biggest thing they learned or to make a public commitment. Encourage boldness as they seek to experience PURE FREEDOM!